JAZZ JAM SESSION

15 Tracks Including Rhythm Changes, Blues, Bossa, Ballads & More

BY ED FRIEDLAND

ISBN 978-1-4234-6569-0

HAL•LEONARD®
CORPORATION
7777 W. BLUEMOUND RD. P.O. BOX 13819 MILWAUKEE, WI 53213

In Australia Contact:
Hal Leonard Australia Pty. Ltd.
4 Lentara Court
Cheltenham, Victoria, 3192 Australia
Email: ausadmin@halleonard.com.au

Visit Hal Leonard Online at
www.halleonard.com

About This Book

Welcome to *Jazz Jam Session*. The progressions contained in this book/CD package belong to standard tunes that are frequently called at a typical jazz jam session (hence the title). They are presented in their standard keys, and with a little detective work on your part, can be found in the Hal Leonard *Real Book Volume 1 Sixth Edition*.

THANKS

I'd like to thank Red Young on piano, and J.J. Johnson on drums for contributing their talents to this project, I think you'll enjoy playing with them as much as I did. Special thanks to Sam Lipman who played tenor sax at the recording session for the benefit of the rhythm section, but sadly is not heard on these tracks.

THE TRACKS

The tracks were performed in typical jazz format, the first and last choruses are where the "head" or melody are played—everything that happens in between is for blowing (improvising). You will hear the drummer count off each tune, and endings will be simple, and stock. Listen for the occasional triple tag of the last 4 bars, or a short ending, a "Count Basie" ending, or the classic "Take The 'A' Train" ending. The first time through each track, it will be a surprise, but it won't be hard to identify what happens after that.

ABOUT THE IMPROV ETUDES

Each tune is paired with an Improv Etude on the page directly facing it, or on the same page. This is included to help you find the melodic material that will fit the tune. They are not intended to be solos for you to mimic on the gig, but they do contain much valuable information. Keep in mind that the information presented in each etude is just one approach to the tune—there are many other ways to understand these songs.

The written lines are a steady stream of eighth notes, which may not sit well with horn players that like to breathe once in a while, but remember—these examples intend to show you as much information as possible within a short timeframe. In addition to the written line, I've included a basic analysis of where these ideas come from. Key centers are notated underneath—"G Maj." for example. This implies that all modes (scales) and arpeggios from that key are workable in those measures. Often you will see a minor key represented like "C Harm. Min." (C Harmonic Minor). This indicates that scales and arpeggios from that key are used. Once in a while, you may see a specific scale mentioned, like "G Sym. Dim." (symmetrical diminished) or "G Whole Tone". If you are not familiar with the modes and arpeggios from the Major, Melodic Minor and Harmonic Minor scales, it's time for you to get to work on that material. It is nearly impossible to make musical sense of jazz without understanding this information.

Other musical devices like chromatic approach notes are used, and are designated by the letters "chr" underneath them. You may notice that in most cases, chromatic approach notes fall on the upbeats, or "ands" of the measure, and lead into a scale or chord tone. Another common technique used in the examples is the indirect resolution, marked with "indir. res." and a bracket. The first note in the bracket is the starting point, and the last note is the intended target of the pattern.

I suggest you listen to the tracks once, then start working your way through the etudes slowly. Most likely, you won't be able to sight read it in tempo the first time… if you can, good work! Remember, these etudes are meant for you to dissect and digest in pieces—they will not serve as a pre-made solo, but there are many ideas contained that are classic to the style.

Best of luck, and keep it swinging!

Ed Friedland

Contents

OLIVE ME

A **Medium Swing**

Cmaj7   E7

A7   Dm7

E7   Am7

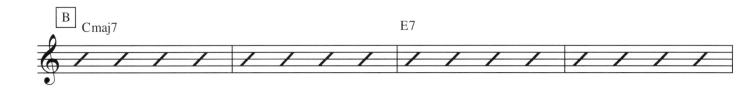

D7   Dm7   G7

B Cmaj7   E7

A7   Dm7

Fmaj7   Fm7   Cmaj7   A7

Dm7   G7   Cmaj7   Am7   Dm7   G7

OLIVE ME – IMPROV ETUDE

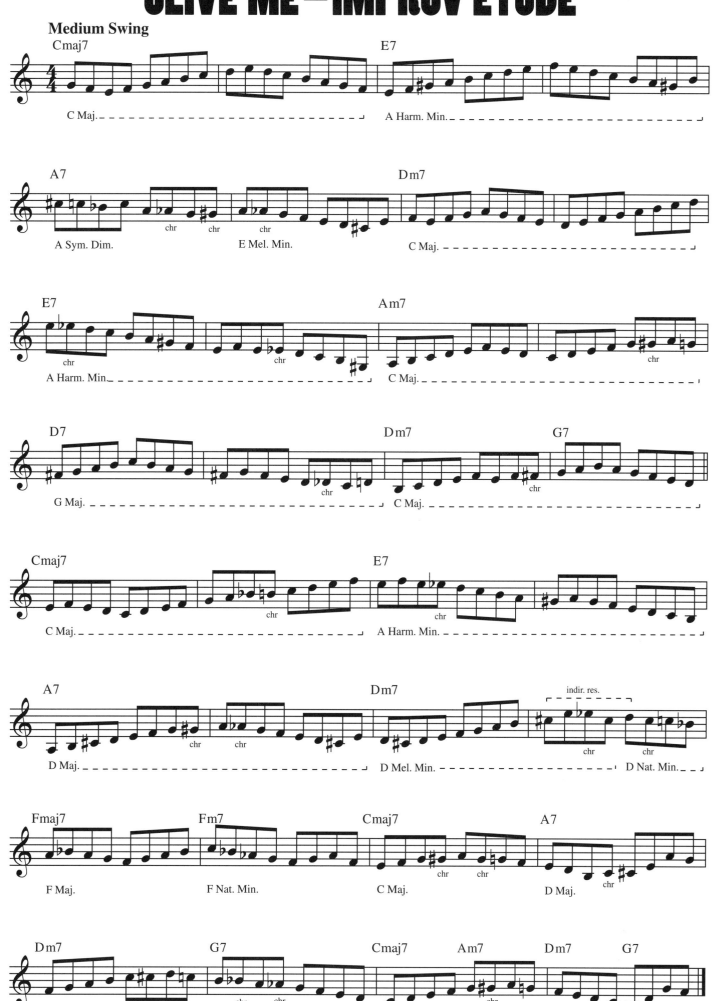

WONDERFUL GLOVE

A **Moderately**

Em7(♭5)   A7(♯5)   Dm

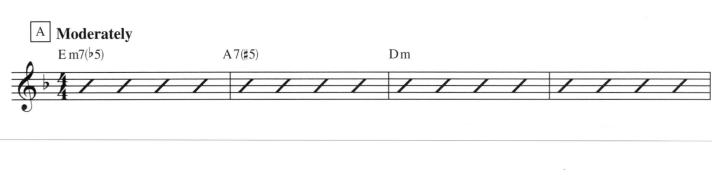

Gm7   C7   Fmaj7   Em7(♭5)   A7

Dm   Gm7   B♭7(♯11)   A7

Dm   G7(♯11)   Em7(♭5)   A7

B Em7(♭5)   A7   Dm

Gm7   C7   Fmaj7   Em7(♭5)   A7

Dm   Gm7   B♭7(♯11)   A7

Dm   B7(♯9)   B♭7   A7   Dm

WONDERFUL GLOVE — IMPROV ETUDE

AIREBIL

Bebop

| Fm7 | C7♯9 | Fm7 | F7 |

| B♭m7 | F7♯9 | B♭m7 | |

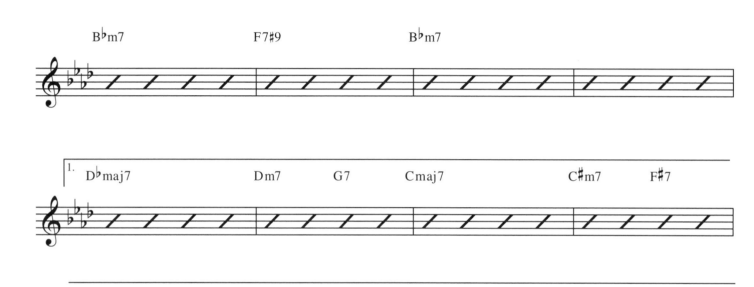

| 1. D♭maj7 | Dm7 G7 | Cmaj7 | C♯m7 F♯7 |

| Bmaj7 | Cm7 F7 | B♭maj7 | |

| B♭m7 | E♭7 | A♭maj7 | Gm7♭5 C7♭9 |

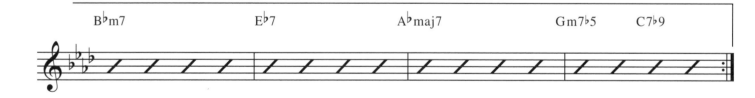

| 2. D♭maj7 | Dm7 G7 | Cm7♭5 | F7 |

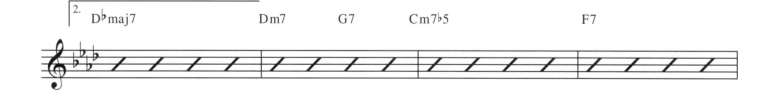

| B♭m7 | E♭7 | A♭maj7 | Gm7♭5 C7♭9 |

AIREBIL – IMPROV ETUDE

Track 4

DONNELY

A Uptempo

Abmaj7   F7   Bb7

Bbm7   Ebmaj7   Abmaj7   Ebm7   Ab7

Dbmaj7   Dbm7   Abmaj7   F7

Bb7   Bbm7   Eb7

B

Abmaj7   F7   Bb7

Gm7b5   C7b9   Fm7   C7

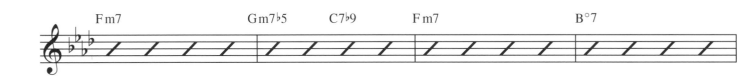
Fm7   Gm7b5   C7b9   Fm7   B°7

Cm7   F7   Bbm7   Eb7   Abmaj7   Bbm7   Eb7

DONNELY – IMPROV ETUDE

Track 5

ALICE'S BLUES

Medium Swing

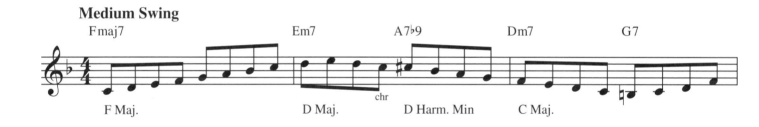

ALICE'S BLUES—IMPROV ETUDE

Medium Swing

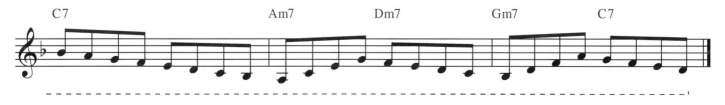

MR. MAC

MR. MAC — IMPROV ETUDE

SPRING IS JUMPIN'

Medium Jazz Waltz

| B♭maj7 | G7♯5 | Cm7 | F7 |

| Gm7 | Fm7 | Em7 | A7 |

| Dm7 | E♭m7 | Dm7 | E♭m7 |

1.
| Bm7♭5 | E7 | Cm7♭5 | F7 |

2.
| Cm7 | F7 | B♭maj7 | Am7♭5   D7 |

| Gm7 | C7 | Fmaj7 | Dm7 |

| A♭m7 | D♭7 | Cm7 | F7 |

| B♭maj7 | G7♯5 | Cm7 | F7 |

| Gm7 | Fm7 | Em7 | A7 |

| Dm7 | E♭m7 | Dm7 | E♭m7 |

| Cm7 | F7 | B♭maj7 (Bmaj7 head only) | B♭maj7 |

SPRING IS JUMPIN' – IMPROV ETUDE

Medium Jazz Waltz

Track 8

MAIN STREET

Uptempo

MAIN STREET – IMPROV ETUDE

MY RAINDANCE

Track 9

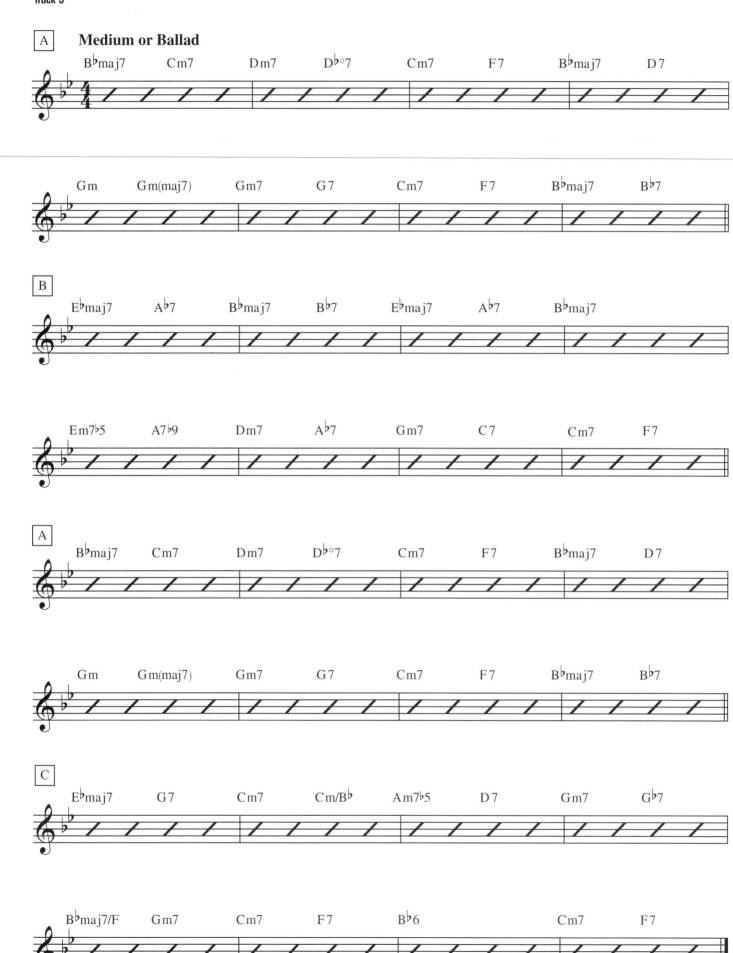

MY RAINDANCE—IMPROV ETUDE

RHYTHM CHANGES

RHYTHM CHANGES — IMPROV ETUDE

Track 11

G BABY

A · **Slow Blues**

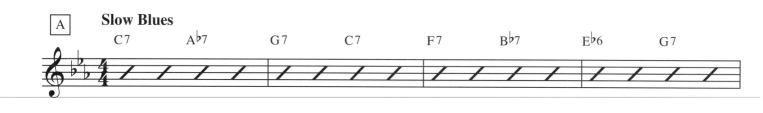

| C7 | A♭7 | G7 | C7 | F7 | B♭7 | E♭6 | G7 |

| C7 | A♭7 | G7 | C7 | F7 | B♭7 | E♭6 | E♭7 |

B

| A♭6 | A°7 | E♭6/B♭ | E♭7 | A♭6 | A°7 | Dm7(♭5) | G7 |

A

| C7 | A♭7 | G7 | C7 | F7 | B♭7 | E♭6 | (A♭7 G7) |

G BABY – IMPROV ETUDE

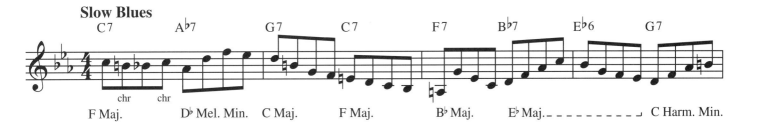

HAVE WE MET?

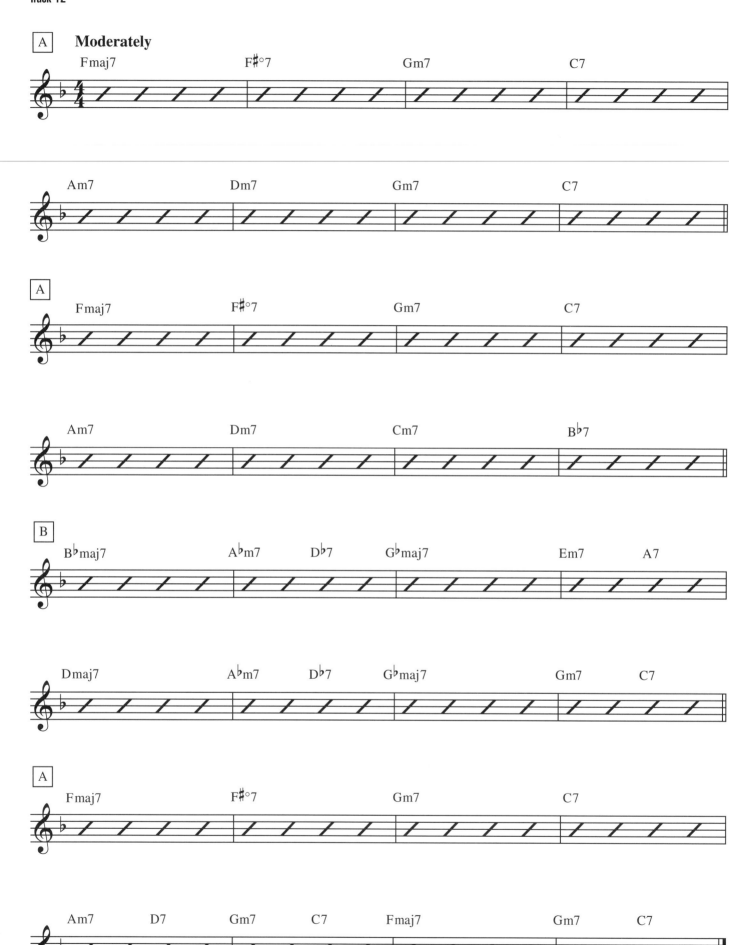

HAVE WE MET? – IMPROV ETUDE

NO GREATER GLOVES

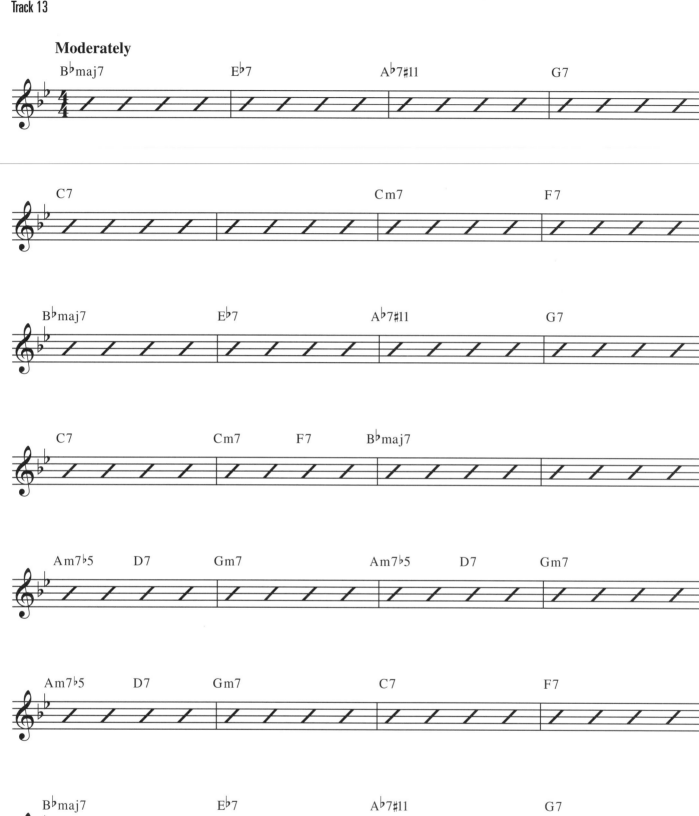

NO GREATER GLOVES — IMPROV ETUDE

INTO SOMEWHERE

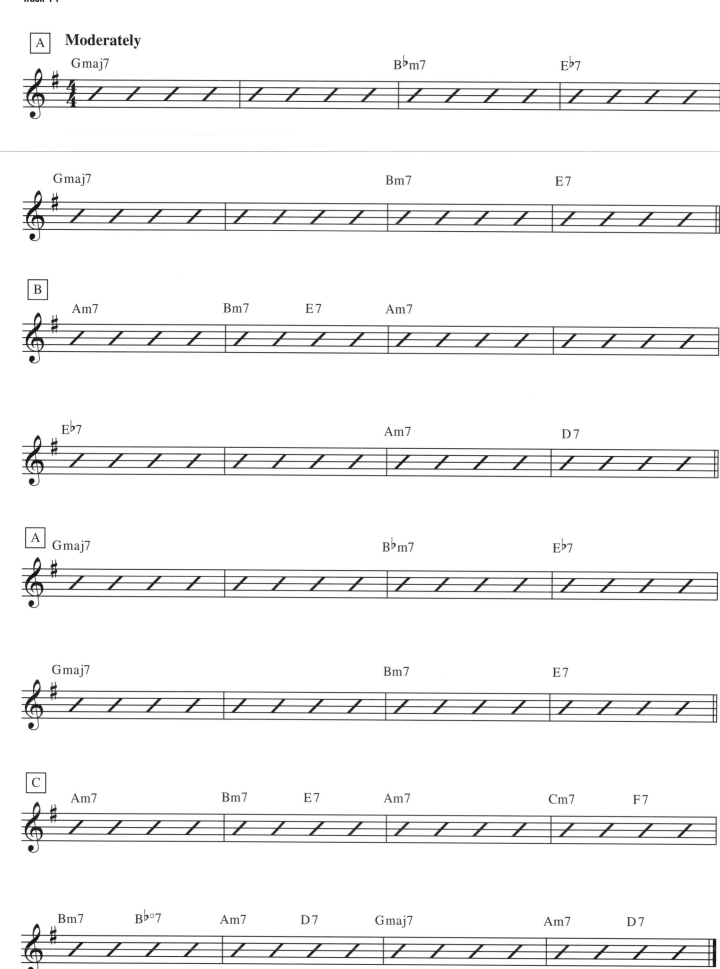

INTO SOMEWHERE — IMPROV ETUDE

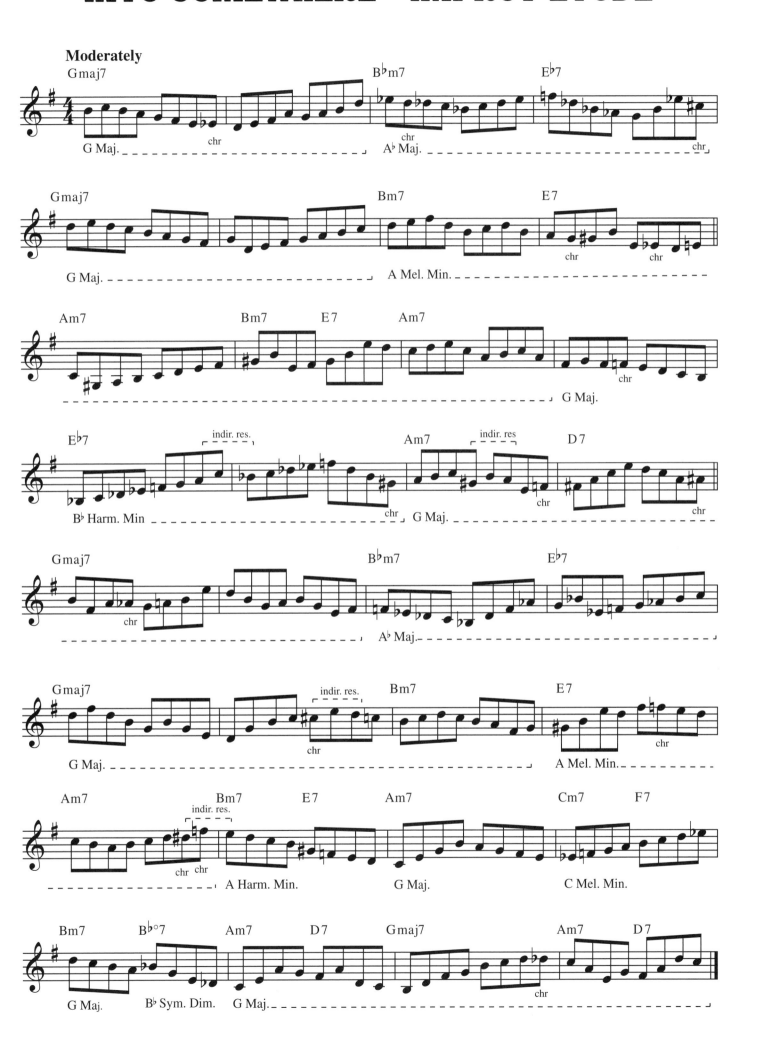

BEE FLAT BLUES

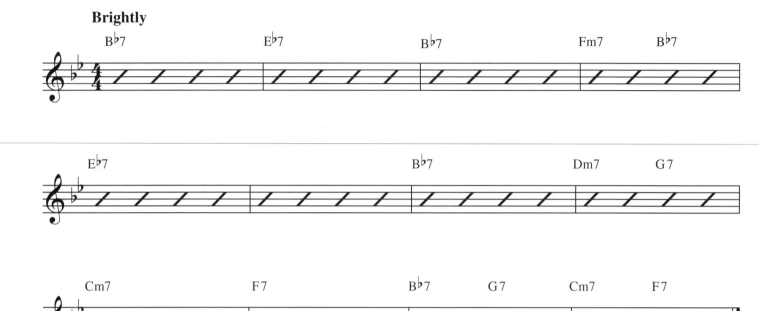

BEE FLAT BLUES—IMPROV ETUDE

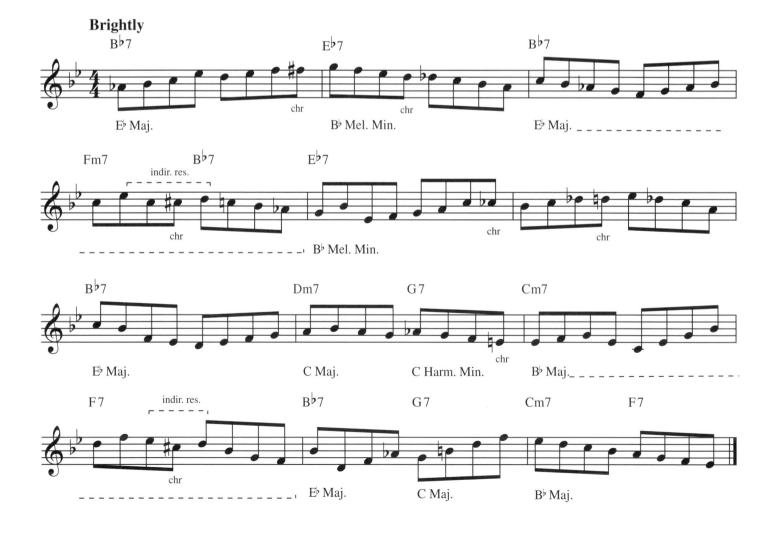

Presenting the Hal Leonard JAZZ PLAY-ALONG® SERIES

1. DUKE ELLINGTON
00841644 ....$16.95

2. MILES DAVIS
00841645 ....$16.95

3. THE BLUES
00841646 ....$16.99

4. JAZZ BALLADS
00841691 ....$16.99

5. BEST OF BEBOP
00841689 ....$16.99

6. JAZZ CLASSICS WITH EASY CHANGES
00841690 ....$16.99

7. ESSENTIAL JAZZ STANDARDS
00843000 ....$16.99

8. ANTONIO CARLOS JOBIM AND THE ART OF THE BOSSA NOVA
00843001 ....$16.95

9. DIZZY GILLESPIE
00843002 ....$16.99

10. DISNEY CLASSICS
00843003 ....$16.99

11. RODGERS AND HART – FAVORITES
00843004 ....$16.99

12. ESSENTIAL JAZZ CLASSICS
00843005 ....$16.99

13. JOHN COLTRANE
00843006 ....$16.95

14. IRVING BERLIN
00843007 ....$15.99

15. RODGERS & HAMMERSTEIN
00843008 ....$15.99

16. COLE PORTER
00843009 ....$15.95

17. COUNT BASIE
00843010 ....$16.95

18. HAROLD ARLEN
00843011 ....$16.95

19. COOL JAZZ
00843012 ....$15.95

20. CHRISTMAS CAROLS
00843080 ....$14.95

21. RODGERS AND HART – CLASSICS
00843014 ....$14.95

22. WAYNE SHORTER
00843015 ....$16.95

23. LATIN JAZZ
00843016 ....$16.95

24. EARLY JAZZ STANDARDS
00843017 ....$14.95

25. CHRISTMAS JAZZ
00843018 ....$16.95

26. CHARLIE PARKER
00843019 ....$16.95

27. GREAT JAZZ STANDARDS
00843020 ....$15.99

28. BIG BAND ERA
00843021 ....$15.99

29. LENNON AND McCARTNEY
00843022 ....$16.95

30. BLUES' BEST
00843023 ....$15.99

31. JAZZ IN THREE
00843024 ....$15.99

32. BEST OF SWING
00843025 ....$15.99

33. SONNY ROLLINS
00843029 ....$15.95

34. ALL TIME STANDARDS
00843030 ....$15.99

35. BLUESY JAZZ
00843031 ....$15.99

36. HORACE SILVER
00843032 ....$16.99

37. BILL EVANS
00843033 ....$16.95

38. YULETIDE JAZZ
00843034 ....$16.95

39. "ALL THE THINGS YOU ARE" & MORE JEROME KERN SONGS
00843035 ....$15.99

40. BOSSA NOVA
00843036 ....$15.99

41. CLASSIC DUKE ELLINGTON
00843037 ....$16.99

42. GERRY MULLIGAN – FAVORITES
00843038 ....$16.99

43. GERRY MULLIGAN – CLASSICS
00843039 ....$16.95

44. OLIVER NELSON
00843040 ....$16.95

45. JAZZ AT THE MOVIES
00843041 ....$15.99

46. BROADWAY JAZZ STANDARDS
00843042 ....$15.99

47. CLASSIC JAZZ BALLADS
00843043 ....$15.99

48. BEBOP CLASSICS
00843044 ....$16.99

49. MILES DAVIS – STANDARDS
00843045 ....$16.95

50. GREAT JAZZ CLASSICS
00843046 ....$15.99

51. UP-TEMPO JAZZ
00843047 ....$15.99

52. STEVIE WONDER
00843048 ....$15.95

53. RHYTHM CHANGES
00843049 ....$15.99

54. "MOONLIGHT IN VERMONT" & OTHER GREAT STANDARDS
00843050 ....$15.99

55. BENNY GOLSON
00843052 ....$15.95

56. "GEORGIA ON MY MIND" & OTHER SONGS BY HOAGY CARMICHAEL
00843056 ....$15.99

57. VINCE GUARALDI
00843057 ....$16.99

58. MORE LENNON AND McCARTNEY
00843059 ....$15.99

59. SOUL JAZZ
00843060 ....$15.99

60. DEXTER GORDON
00843061 ....$15.95

61. MONGO SANTAMARIA
00843062 ....$15.95

62. JAZZ-ROCK FUSION
00843063 ....$14.95

63. CLASSICAL JAZZ
00843064 ....$14.95

64. TV TUNES
00843065 ....$14.95

65. SMOOTH JAZZ
00843066 ....$16.99

66. A CHARLIE BROWN CHRISTMAS
00843067 ....$16.99

67. CHICK COREA
00843068 ....$15.95

68. CHARLES MINGUS
00843069 ....$16.95

69. CLASSIC JAZZ
00843071 ....$15.99

70. THE DOORS
00843072 ....$14.95

71. COLE PORTER CLASSICS
00843073 ....$14.95

72. CLASSIC JAZZ BALLADS
00843074 ....$15.99

73. JAZZ/BLUES
00843075 ....$14.95

74. BEST JAZZ CLASSICS
00843076 ....$15.99

75. PAUL DESMOND
00843077 ....$14.95

76. BROADWAY JAZZ BALLADS
00843078 ....$15.99

77. JAZZ ON BROADWAY
00843079 ....$15.99

78. STEELY DAN
00843070 ....$15.99

79. MILES DAVIS – CLASSICS
00843081 ....$15.99

80. JIMI HENDRIX
00843083 ....$15.99

81. FRANK SINATRA – CLASSICS
00843084 ....$15.99

82. FRANK SINATRA – STANDARDS
00843085 ....$15.99

83. ANDREW LLOYD WEBBER
00843104 ....$14.95

84. BOSSA NOVA CLASSICS
00843105 ....$14.95

85. MOTOWN HITS
00843109 ....$14.95

86. BENNY GOODMAN
00843110 ....$14.95

87. DIXIELAND
00843111 ....$14.9⁹

88. DUKE ELLINGTON FAVORITES
00843112 ....$14.9

89. IRVING BERLIN FAVORITES
00843113 ....$14.9

90. THELONIOUS MONK CLASSICS
00841262 ....$16.9⁹

91. THELONIOUS MONK FAVORITES
00841263 ....$16.9⁹

93. DISNEY FAVORITES
00843142 ....$14.9⁹

94. RAY
00843143 ....$14.9

95. JAZZ AT THE LOUNGE
00843144 ....$14.9

96. LATIN JAZZ STANDARDS
00843145 ....$14.9⁹

98. DAVE FRISHBERG
00843149 ....$14.9⁹

105. SOULFUL JAZZ
00843151 ....$14.9⁹

106. SLO' JAZZ
00843117 ....$14.9⁹

107. MOTOWN CLASSICS
00843116 ....$14.9⁹

The Hal Leonard JAZZ PLAY-ALONG® SERIES is the ultimate learning tool for all jazz musicians. With musician-friendly lead sheets, melody cues and other split track choices on the included CD, these packs make learning to play jazz easier and more fun than ever before. Parts are included for B♭, E♭, C and Bass Clef instruments.

Prices, contents, and availability subject to change without notice.

FOR MORE INFORMATION, SEE YOUR LOCAL MUSIC DEALER, OR WRITE TO:

HAL•LEONARD®
CORPORATION
7777 W. BLUEMOUND RD. P.O. BOX 13819
MILWAUKEE, WISCONSIN 53213

Visit Hal Leonard online at
www.halleonard.com
for complete songlists.

0109